125+ Funny Jokes for Kids

Johnny B.Laughing

"The Joke King"

DEDICATION

This book is dedicated to the one's out there that love to be silly, have fun, and laugh. It's because of humor that the world keeps spinning..

CONTENTS

1 KNOCK KNOCK JOKES

Knock knock!
Who's there?
Cheese!
Cheese who?
Cheese a cute girl!

Knock knock!
Who's there?
Bacon!
Bacon who?
Bacon a cake for your birthday!

Knock knock!
Who's there?
Burglar!
Burglar who?
Burglars don't knock!

Knock knock!
Who's there?
Cows!
Cows who?
Cows go moo not who!

Knock knock!
Who's there?
Aitch!
Aitch who?
Bless You!

Knock knock!
Who's there?
Carrie!
Carrie who?
Carrie my bag!

Knock knock!
Who's there?
Ben!
Ben who?
Ben waiting for too long!

Knock knock!
Who's there?
Summer!
Summer who?
Summer good and summer bad!

Knock knock!
Who's there?
Cargo!
Cargo who?
Cargo better if you fill it up with gas first!

Knock knock!
Who's there?
Geno!
Geno who?
Geno any good jokes?

Knock knock!
Who's there?
Shelby!
Shelby who?
Shelby coming around the mountain when she comes!

Knock knock!
Who's there?
Read!
Read who?
Read between the lines!

Knock knock!
Who's there?
Edwin!
Edwin who?
Edwin some and you lose some!

Knock knock!
Who's there?
Nadia!
Nadia who?
Nadia head while the music plays!

Knock knock!
Who's there?
Vanna!
Vanna who?
Vanna go see a movie tonight?

Knock knock!
Who's there?
Alfredo!
Alfredo who?
Alfredo the dark! Please open the door!

2 ANIMAL JOKES

Q: What do chickens serve at birthday parties?
A: Coop-cakes!

Q: Why don't chickens like people?
A: They beat eggs!

Q: Why did the chicken cross the basketball court?
A: He heard the referee calling fowls!

Q: What happened when the owl lost his voice?
A: He didn't give a hoot!

Q: Why did the rooster run away?
A: He was chicken!

Q: What kind of doctor does a duck visit?
A: A ducktor!

Q: What is the biggest ant in the world?
A: An elephant!

Q: What kind of suit does a bee wear to work?
A: A buzzness suit!

Q: How do fireflies lose weight?
A: They burn calories.

Q: How do fleas travel?
A: Itch hiking!

Q: Why did the spider buy a car?
A: So he could take it out for a spin!

Q: What did the worm say to the other when he was late home?
A: Where in earth have you been!

Q: What did one firefly say to the other?
A: Got to glow now!

Q: What are the smartest bees?
A: Spelling bees!

Q: What do you call it when a cat stops?
A: A paws!

Q: Why does everyone love cats?
A: They're purr-fect!

Q: Which big cat should you never play cards with?
A: A cheetah!

Q: What does a cat call a bowl of mice?
A: A purrfect meal!

Q: What do you get if you cross a cat with Santa?
A: Santa Claws!

Q: What do you get if you cross a cat with a parrot?
A: A carrot!

Q: Why wouldn't anyone play with the little longhorn?
A: He was too much of a bully!

Q: Why did the farmer fence in the bull?
A: The farmer had too much of a steak in him to let him go!

Q: Where do Russian cows come from?
A: Moscow!

Q: Where do cows go to dance?
A: To the meat ball!

Q: What's a cow's favorite musical note?
A: Beef-flat!

Q: What happened to the lost cattle?
A: Nobody's herd (heard)!

Q: What do you call a cow that's just had a baby?
A: De-calfinated!

Q: What do you call a sleeping bull?
A: A bull-dozer!

Q: What did one dairy cow say to another?
A: Got milk?

Q: What dinosaur loves pancakes?
A: A tri-syrup-tops!

Q: Why did the dinosaur walk on two legs?
A: To give the ants a chance!

Q: What was the most flexible dinosaur?
A: Tyrannosaurus Flex!

Q: What do you get when you put a bomb and a dinosaur together?
A: Dino-mite!

Q: What vehicle does T-Rex use to go from planet to planet?
A: A Dinosaucer!

Q: What is it called when two dinosaurs get in a wreck?
A: A tyrannosaurus wrecks!

Q: When is a strange dog most likely to walk into your house?
A: When the door is wide open!

Q: Why was the mother flea so unhappy?
A: All her children have gone to the dogs!

Q: Why did the broke leg dog say he was an actor?
A: His leg was in a cast!

Q: Which dog can tell time?
A: A watchdog!

Q: What is black and white and red all over?
A: A Dalmatian with bad sunburn!

Q: What did the dog say when he chased his tail?
A: This is the end!

Q: How do you feel if you cross a sheepdog with a melon?
A: Melon-collie!

Q: What do you get if you cross a computer and a Rottweiler?
A: A computer with a lot of bites!

Q: Why do elephants eat raw food?
A: Because they don't know how to cook!

Q: What kind of elephant lives in Antarctica?
A: A cold one!

Q: What's big and grey and protects you from the rain?
A: An umbrellaphant!

Q: Why do elephants live in the jungle?
A: Because they don't have to pay rent!

Q: How do you raise a baby elephant?
A: With a fork lift truck!

Q: What do you get when you cross an elephant and a rhino?
A: Elephino!

Q: What fish make the best sandwiches?
A: A peanut butter and jellyfish!

Q: Where do fish sleep?
A: In a riverbed!

Q: Why are fish no good at tennis?
A: They don't like to get close to nets!

Q: How do you communicate with a fish?
A: You drop it a line!

Q: Which fish dresses the best?
A: A swordfish because it always looks sharp!

Q: Why is a fish easy to weigh?
A: Because it has its own scales!

Q: Which fish go to heaven when they die?
A: Angelfish!

Q: What do you feed a 600 pound gorilla?
A: Anything it wants!

Q: Why did the gorilla fail English?
A: He had little ape-titude!

Q: Why are gorillas underpaid?
A: They're willing to work for peanuts!

Q: How come the giant ape climbed up the side of the skyscraper?
A: The elevator was broken!

Q: How do you make a gorilla float?
A: Two scoops of ice cream, some soda and a gorilla!

Q: What kind of tie does a pig wear?
A: A pig sty!

Q: What are pigs warned to look out for in New York?
A: Pig pockets!

Q: Why was the pig unhappy in the Minors?
A: Because he wants to play in the Pig Leagues!

Q: Why do pigs like February 14th?
A: They get lots of Valenswines!

Q: Why did the pigs paint their hooves green?
A: It was Saint Pigtrick's Day!

Q: Why did the pig go to the casino?
A: To play the slop machines!

Q: Why are there so many piggy banks?
A: Pigs don't like to hide their money in the mattress!

Q: Who sends flowers on Valentine's Day?
A: Cupigs!

Q: What do you call a pig thief?
A: A hamburglar!

Q: What do you get when you cross a perm with a rabbit?
A: Curly hare!

Q: Why couldn't the rabbit fly home for Easter?
A: He didn't have the hare fare!

Q: Where do rabbits go after their wedding?
A: On their bunnymoon!

Q: What's a rabbit's favorite dance?
A: The bunny hop!

Q: What do you call a rabbit who tells jokes?
A: A funny bunny!

Q: What do you call a rabbit with fleas?
A: Bugs Bunny!

Q: How many skunks do you need to make a house really smelly?
A: Just a phew!

Q: What's a skunk's philosophy on life?
A: Eat, stink, and be merry!

Q: What do you get if you cross a skunk and a wasp?
A: Something that stinks and stings!

Q: What's a skunk's favorite game in school?
A: Show and smell!

Q: Did you hear the joke about the skunk?
A: Never mind, it stinks!

3 PROFESSION JOKES

Q: What do astronauts put on their toast?
A: Space Jam!

Q: Where do astronauts leave their spaceships?
A: At parking meteors!

Q: Which astronaut wears the biggest helmet?
A: The one with the biggest head!

Q: Why didn't the astronauts stay on the moon?
A: Because it was a full moon and there was no room!

Q: Why don't astronauts get hungry after being blasted into space?
A: Because they've just had a big launch!

Q: What did the overweight ballet dancer perform?
A: The dance of the sugar plump fairy!

Q: What dance do you do when summer is over?
A: Tango (tan go)!

Q: What do tired line dancers do?
A: They line down!

Q: Why don't dogs make good dancers?
A: Because they have two left feet!

Q: How do you make a tissue dance?
A: Put a little boogie in it!

Q: Why are false teeth like stars?
A: Because they come out at night!

Q: What helps keep your teeth together?
A: Toothpaste!

Q: Why is a toothless dog like a tree?
A: It has more bark than bite!

Q: What did the tooth say to the dentist?
A: Filler up!

Q: Why does a vampire clean his teeth three times a day?
A: To prevent bat breath!

Q: Why do artists never win when they play soccer?
A: They keep drawing!

Q: What part of a football stadium is never the same?
A: The changing rooms!

Q: Why do managers bring suitcases along to away games?
A: So that they can pack the defense!

Q: What stories are told by basketball players?
A: Tall tales!

Q: What lights up a soccer stadium?
A: A soccer match!

Q: How is a heart like a musician?
A: They both have a beat!

Q: Why did the boy bring a ladder to chorus?
A: He wanted to sing higher!

Q: What do you get if you cross a lamp with a violin?
A: You get light music!

Q: How do you know if there is a drummer at your door?
A: The knocking always speeds up!

Q: Why do bagpipers walk when they play?
A: To get away from the noise!

4 FOOD JOKES

Q: What's the best day to eat bacon?
A: Fry-day!

Q: How do you make gold soup?
A: Put 14 carrots in it!

Q: What looks just like half a loaf of bread?
A: Its other half!

Q: How do you make an apple turnover?
A: Push it downhill!

Q: What food is good for the brain?
A: Noodle soup!

Q: What's a dolls favorite food?
A: Barbie-Q!

Q: Why did the banana go out with the prune?
A: Because he couldn't find a date!

Q: Who are the hamburgers favorite people?
A: Vegetarians!

Q: What do you call a fake noodle?
A: An impasta!

Q: What do you get if you cross an alien and a hot drink?
A: Gravi-tea!

Q: What did one plate say to the other plate?
A: Lunch is on me!

Q: Where does a burger feel at home?
A: On the range!

Q: What is a ghost's favorite fruit?
A: Boonana!

Q: What sort of soup do skeletons like?
A: One with plenty of body in it!

Q: What did one strawberry say to the other?
A: Look at the jam you've gotten us into!

Q: Why aren't burgers too good at basketball?
A: Too many turnovers!

ABOUT THE AUTHOR

The Joke King, Johnny B. Laughing is a best-selling children's joke book author. He is a jokester at heart and enjoys a good laugh, pulling pranks on his friends, and telling funny and hilarious jokes!

For more funny joke books just search for *JOHNNY B. LAUGHING* on Amazon.com

Visit the website:
www.funny-jokes-online.weebly.com